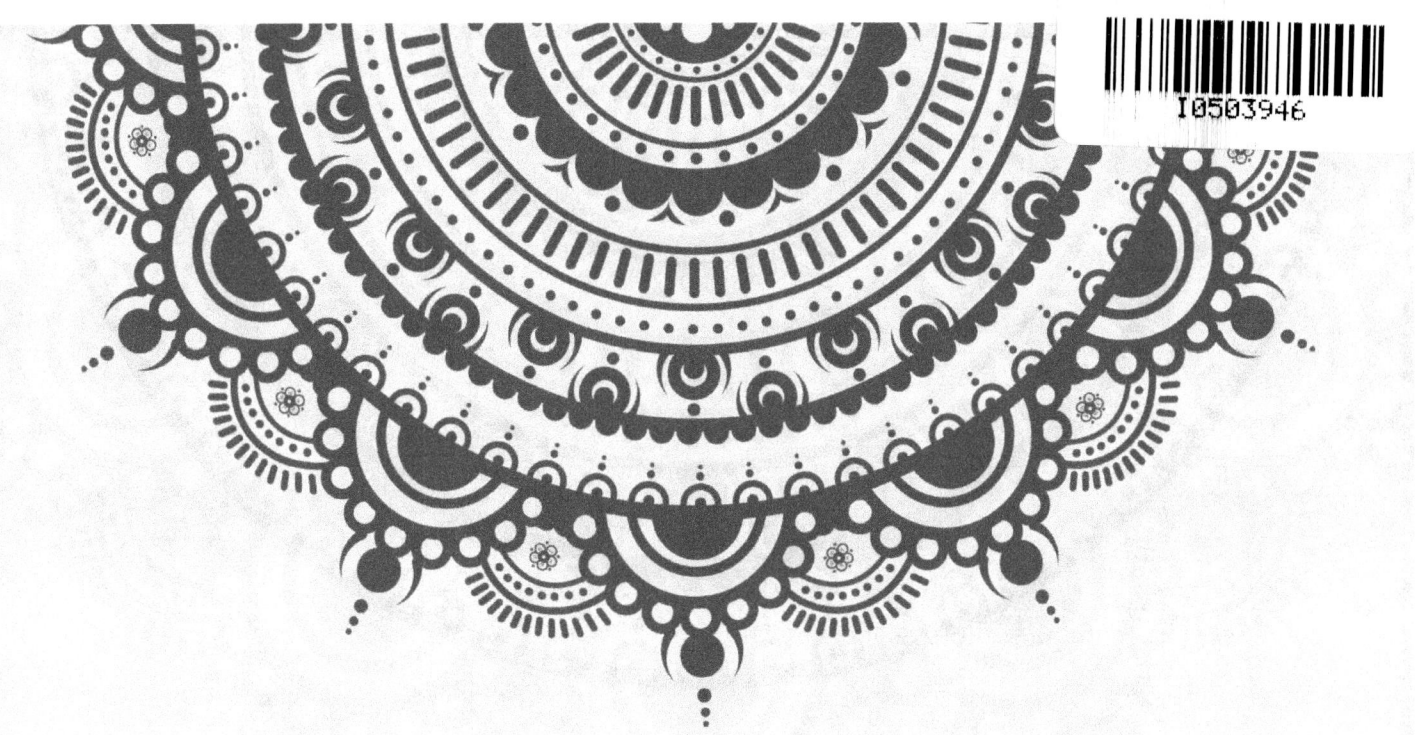

* This books belongs to *

....

....

....

Indian Elephant Mandala

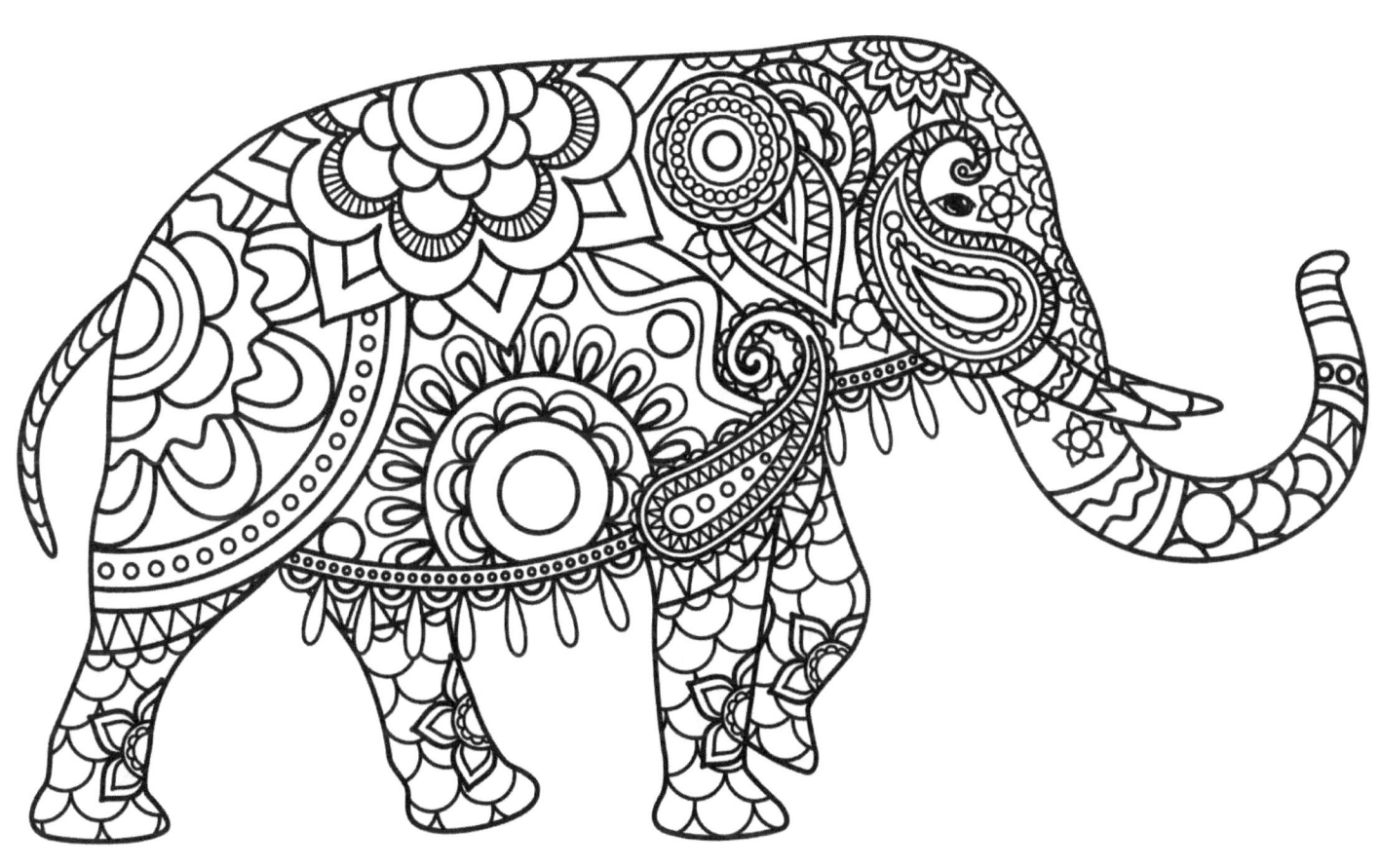

Circular mandala isolated

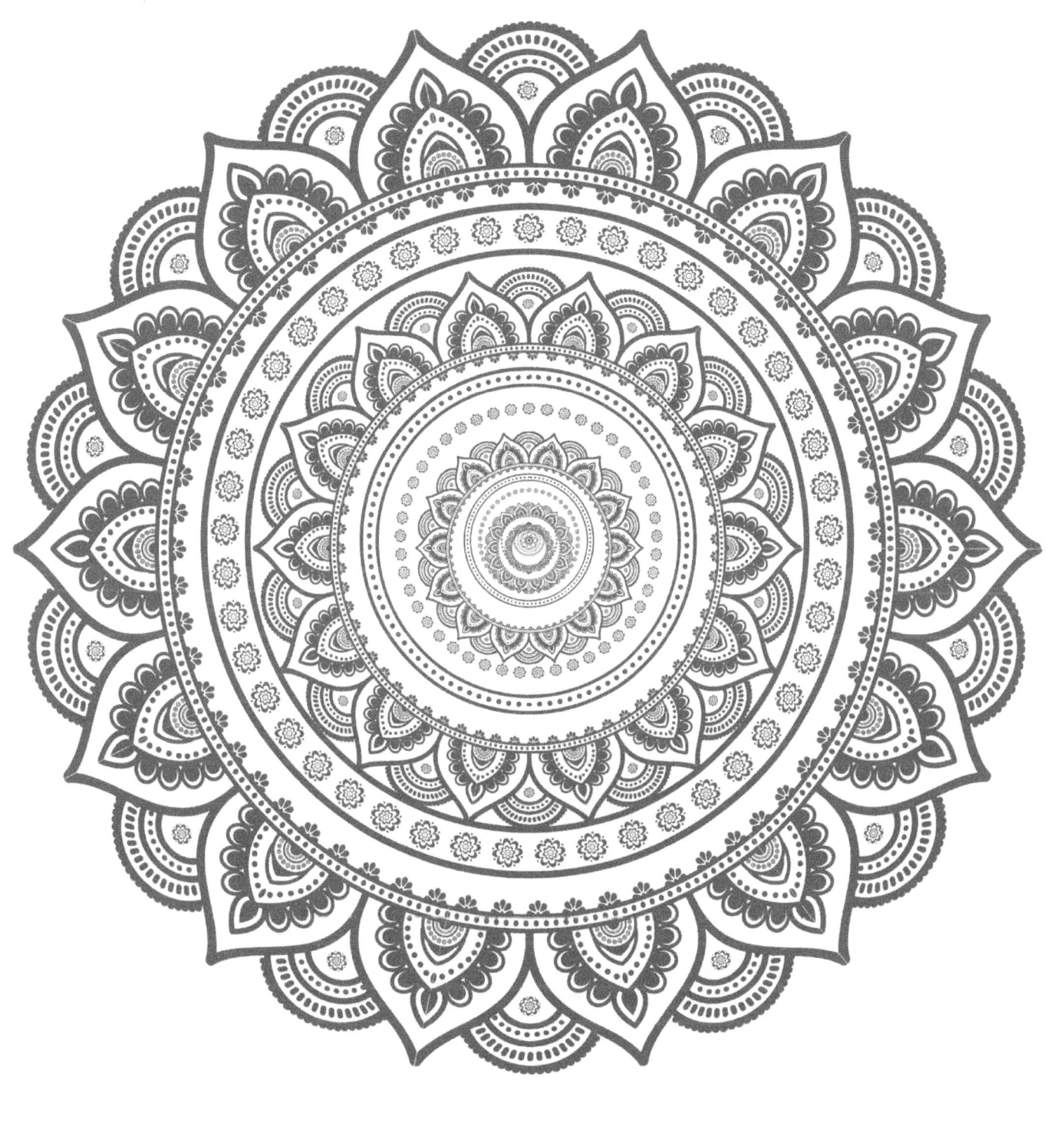

Oriental therapy yoga mandalas

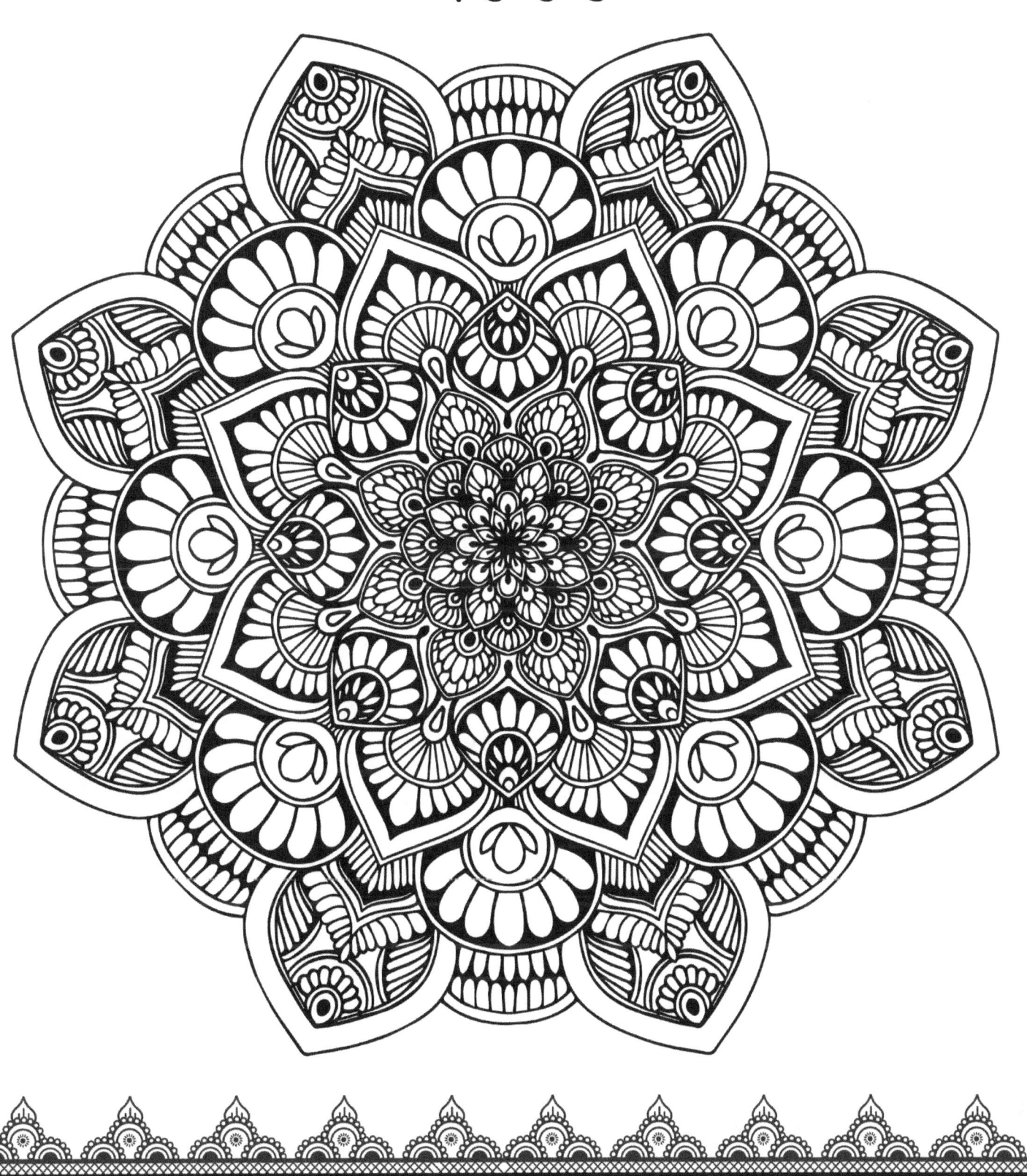

Oriental therapy yoga mandalas

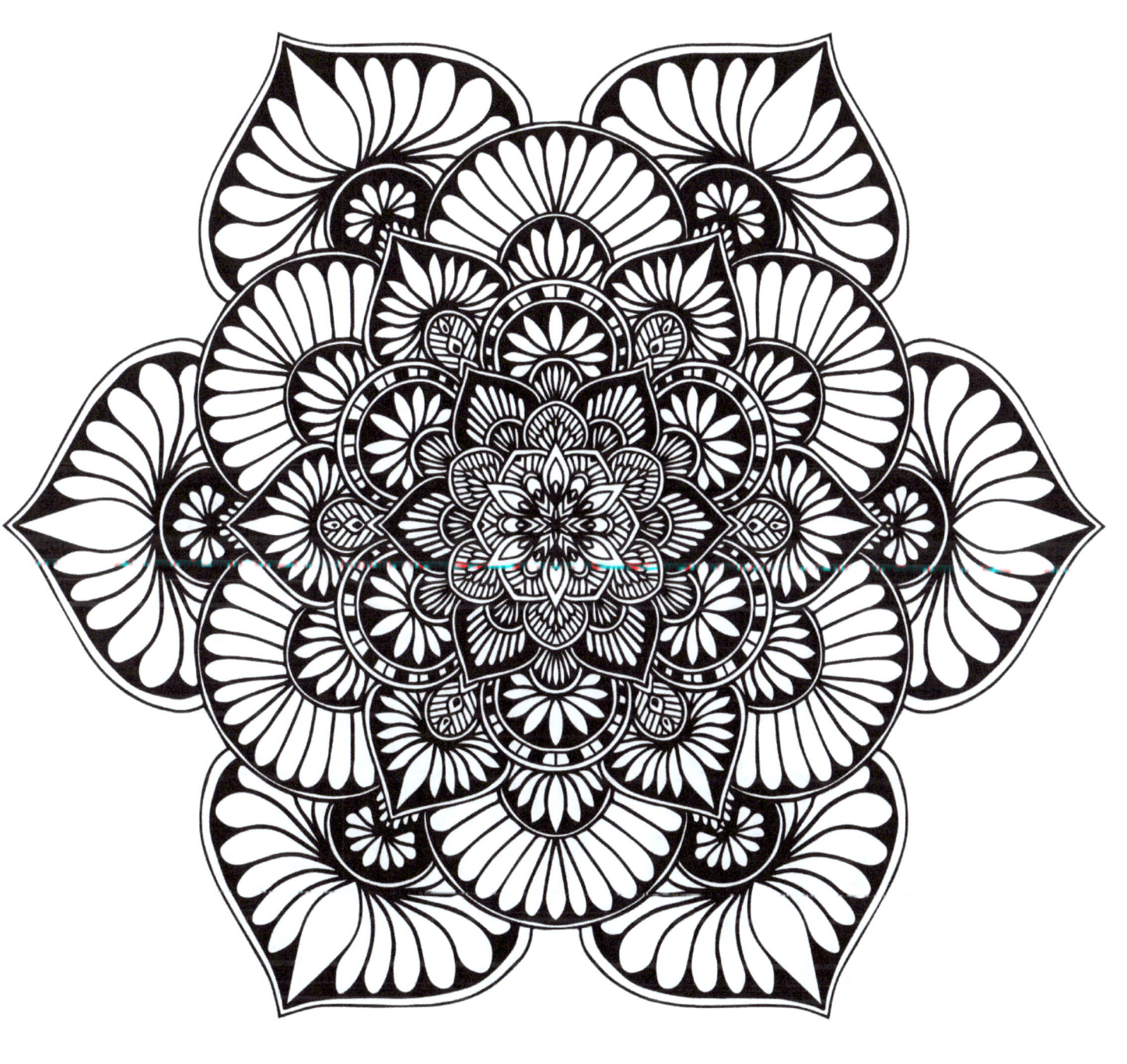

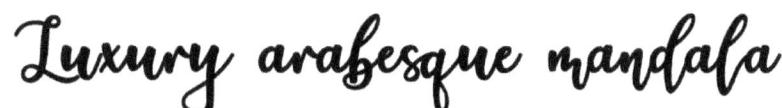

Luxury arabesque mandala

Indian Elephant Mandala

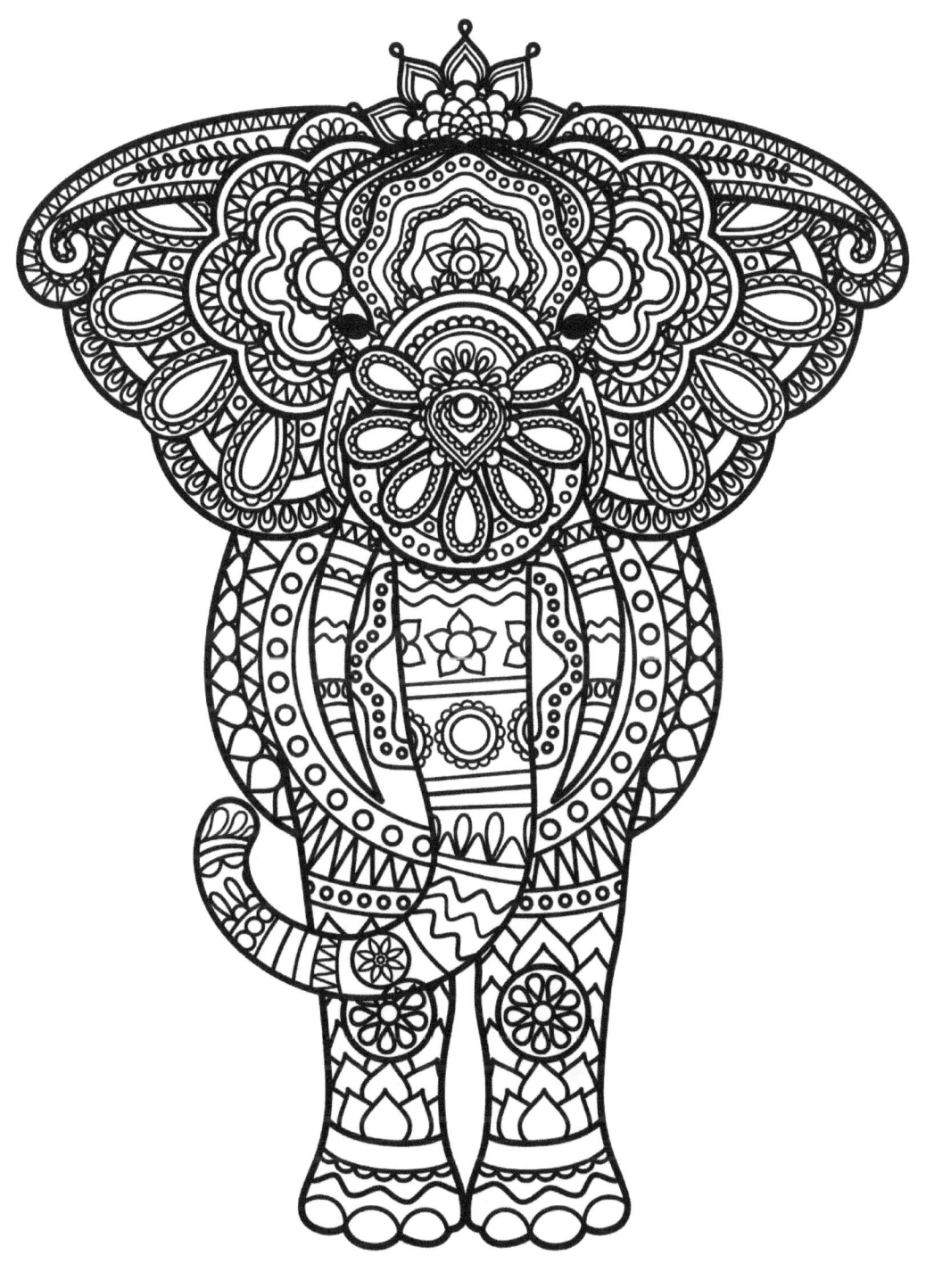

Indian Elephant Mandala

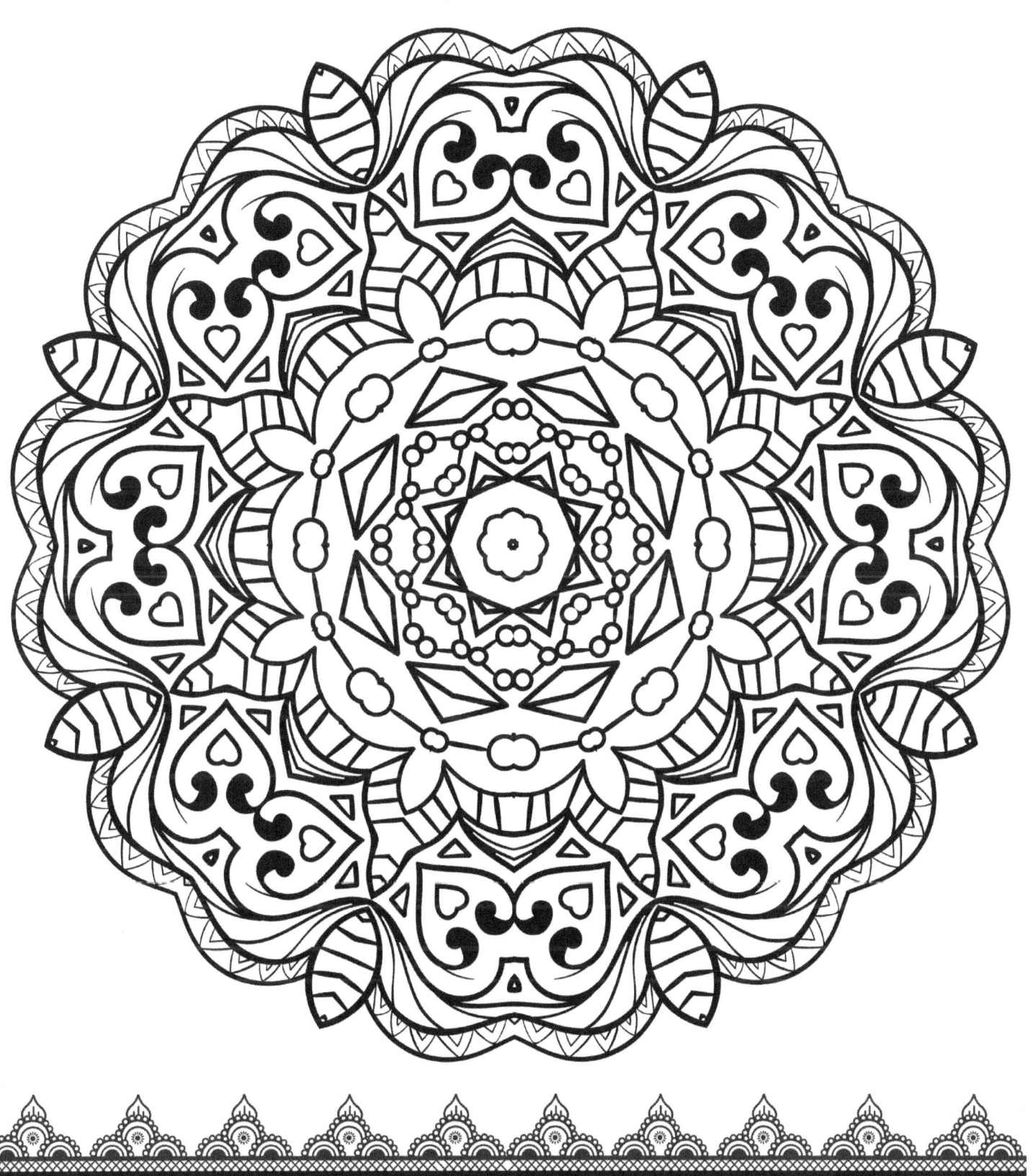

Ethnic fractal mandala meditation

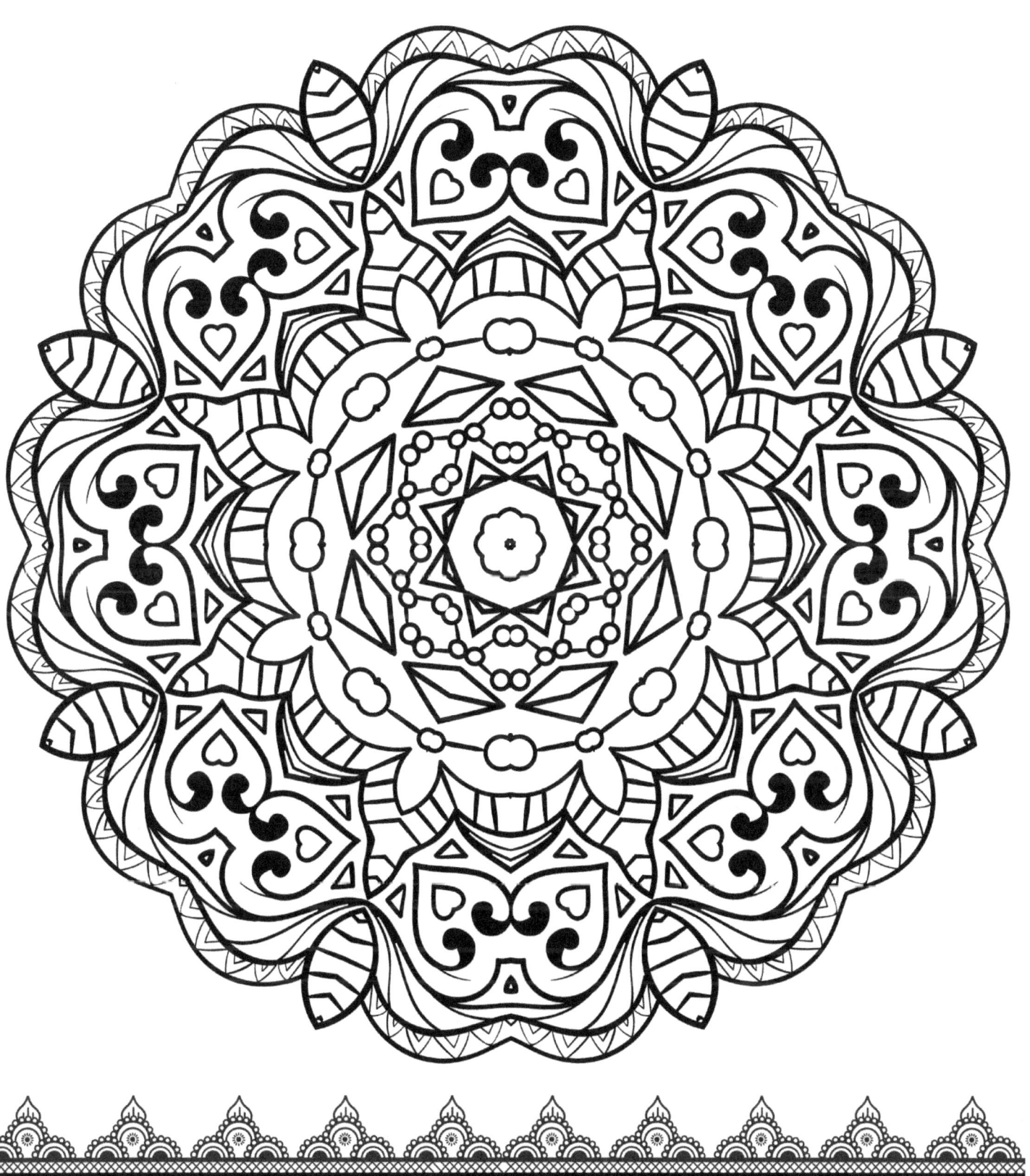

Floral Mandalas

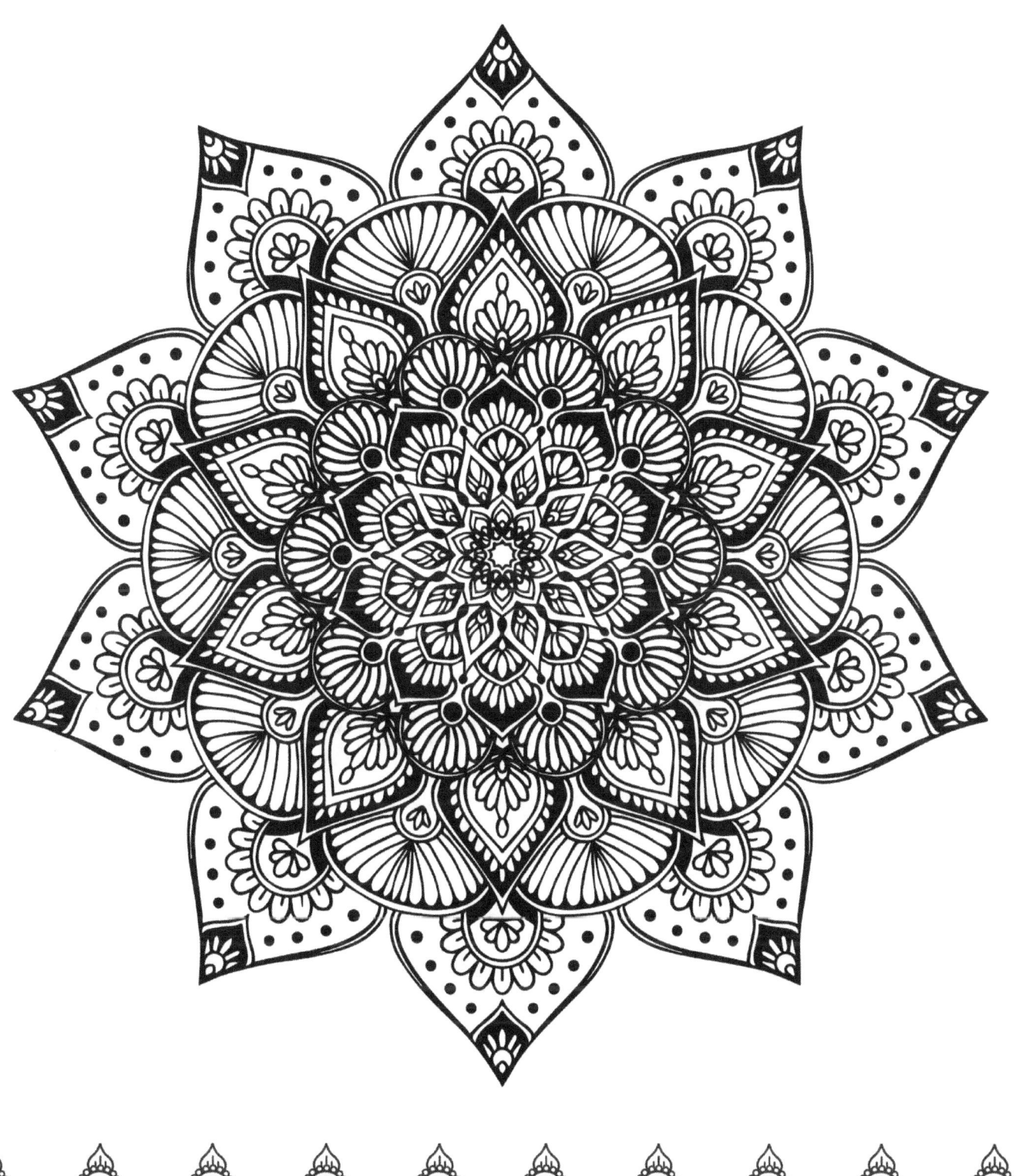

Circle shape pattern with cute birds Mandalas

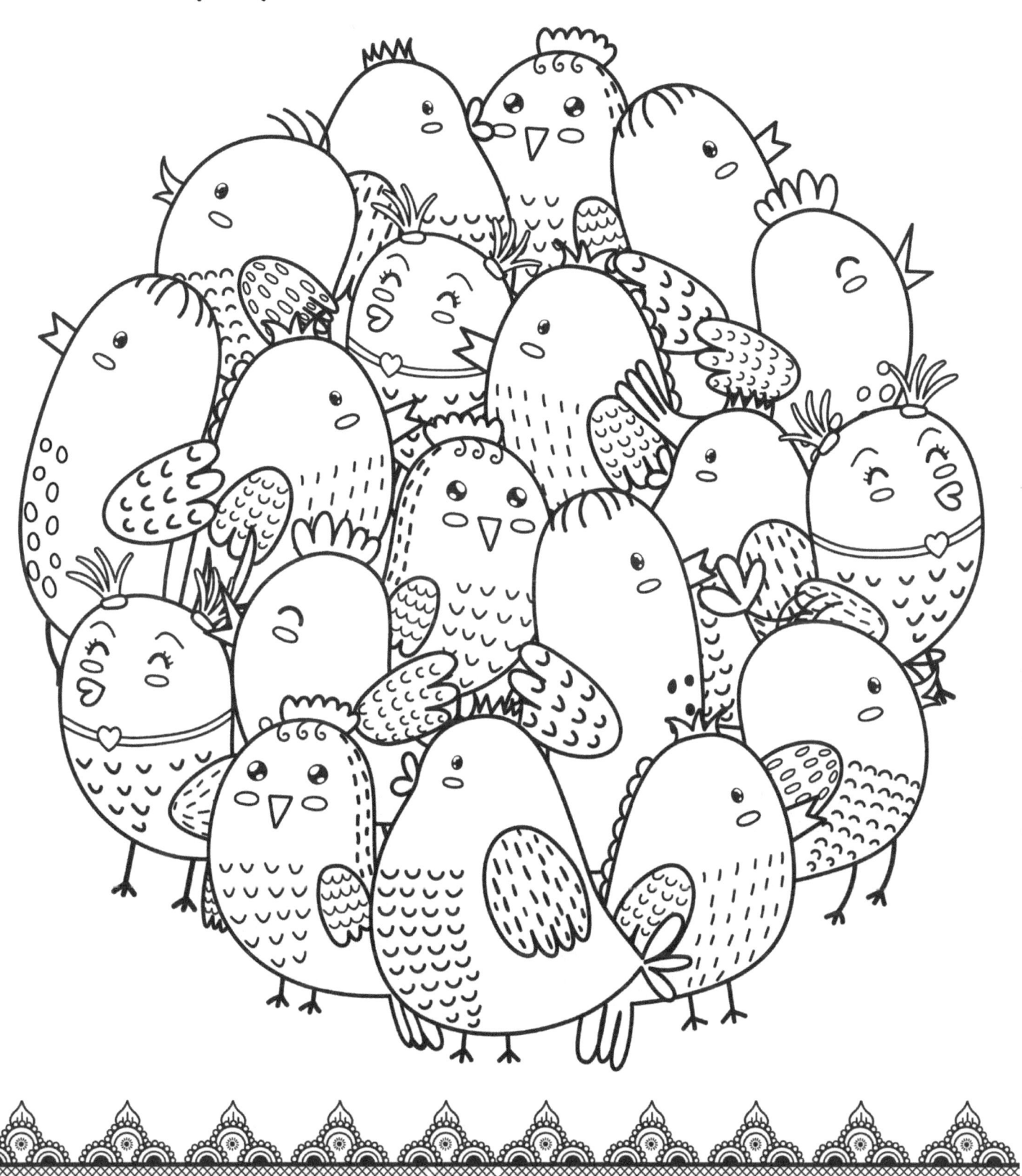

Floral Mandalas

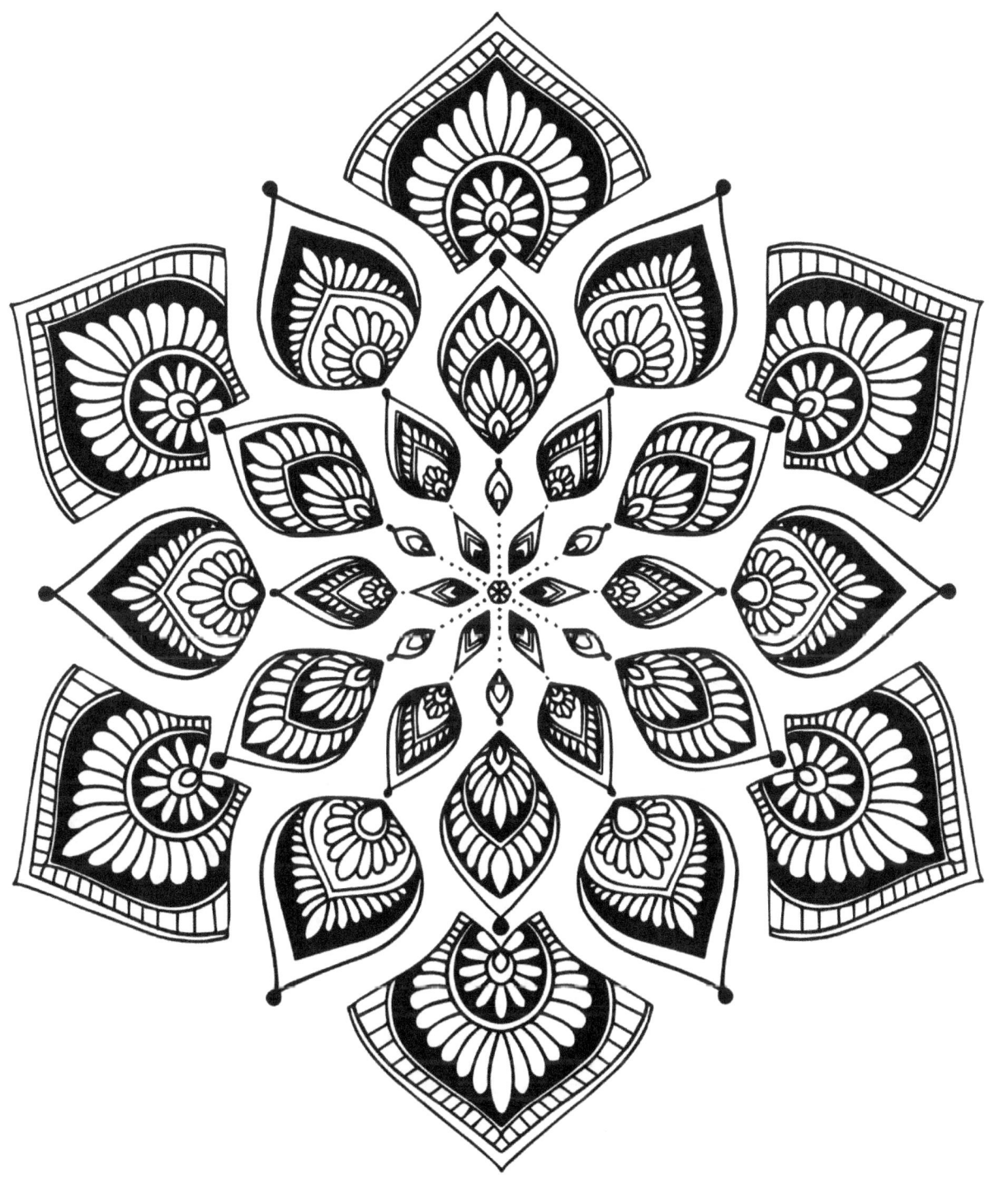

Floral Mandalas

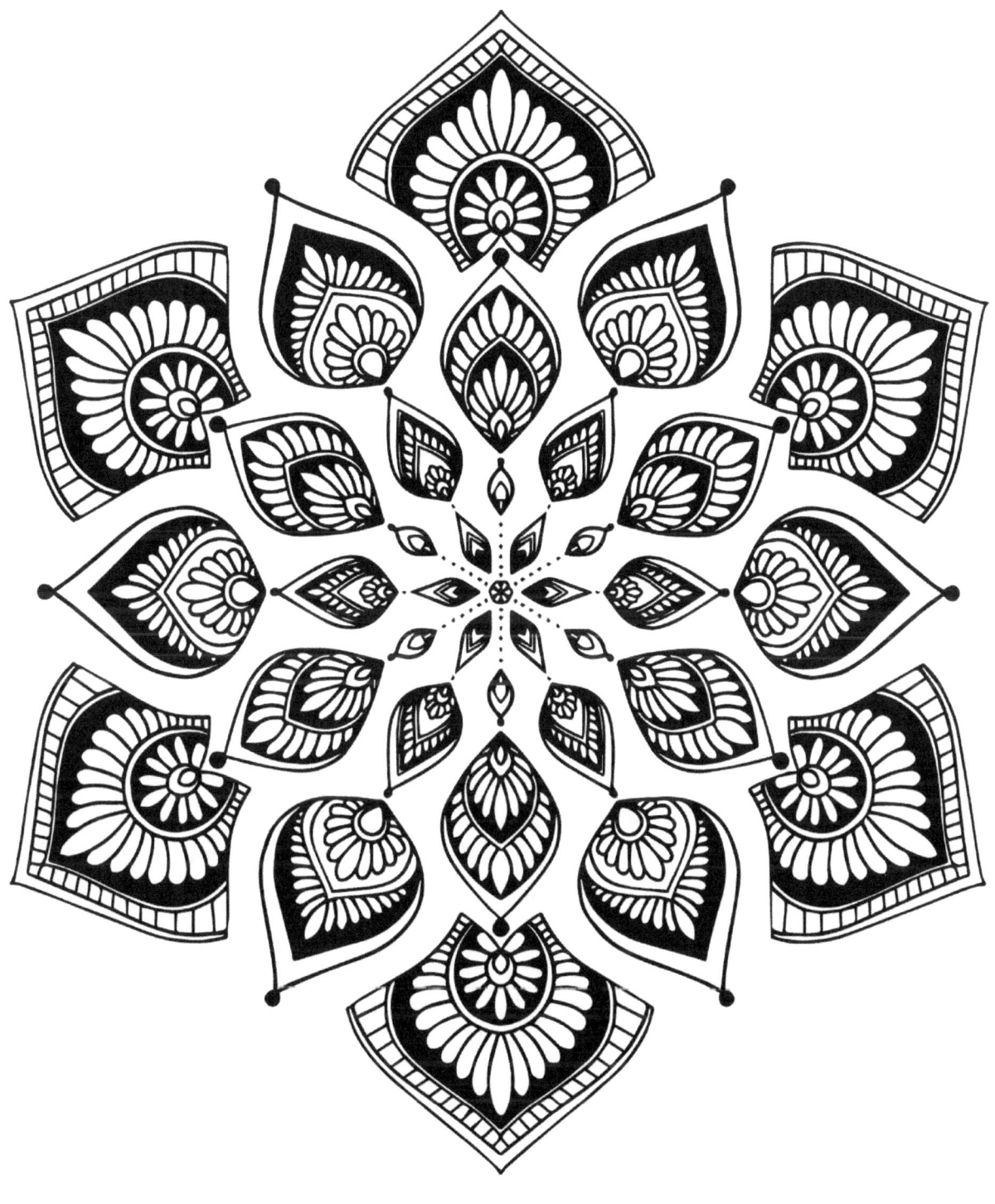

Circular symmetric mandala

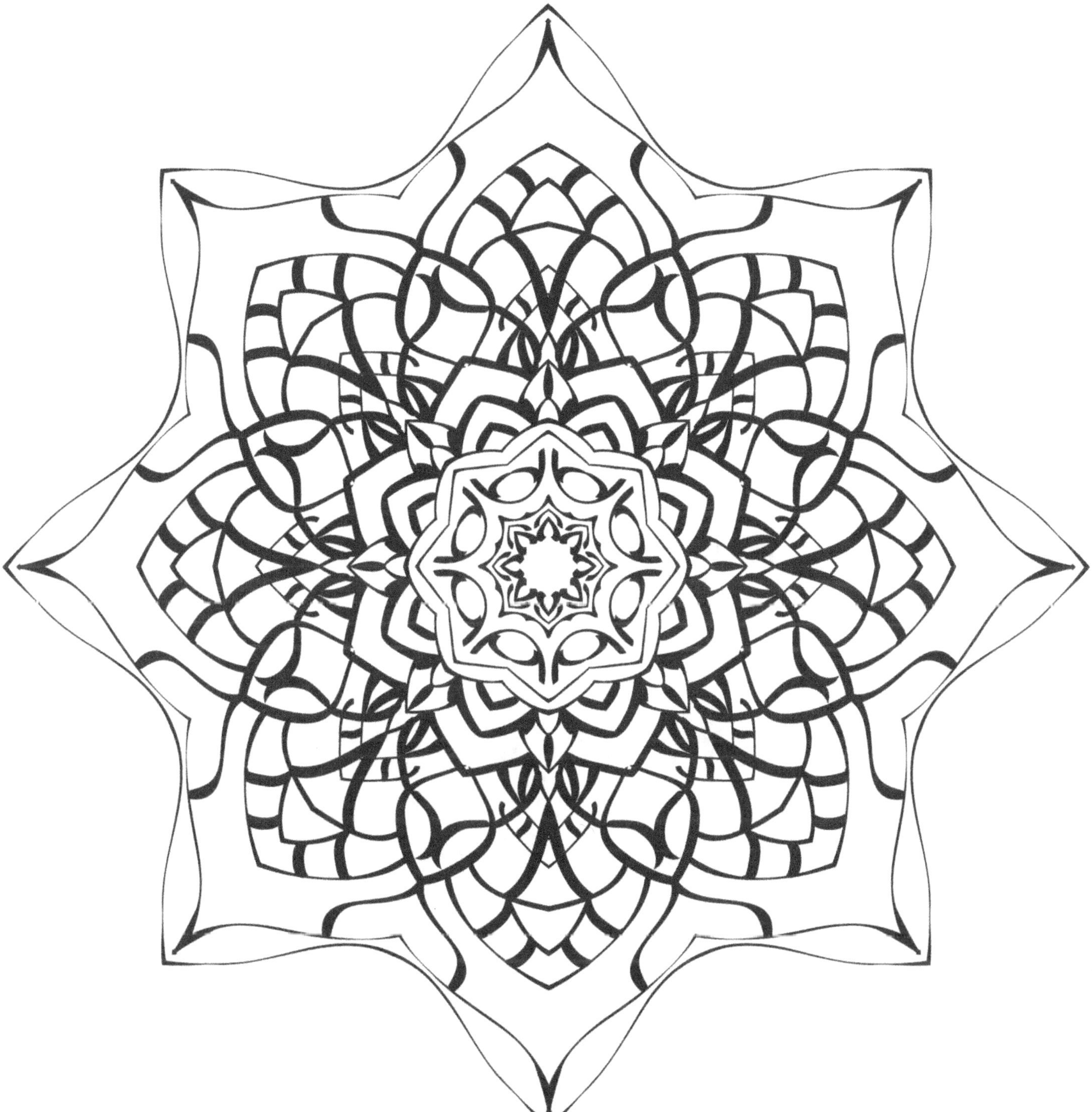

Circular symmetric mandala

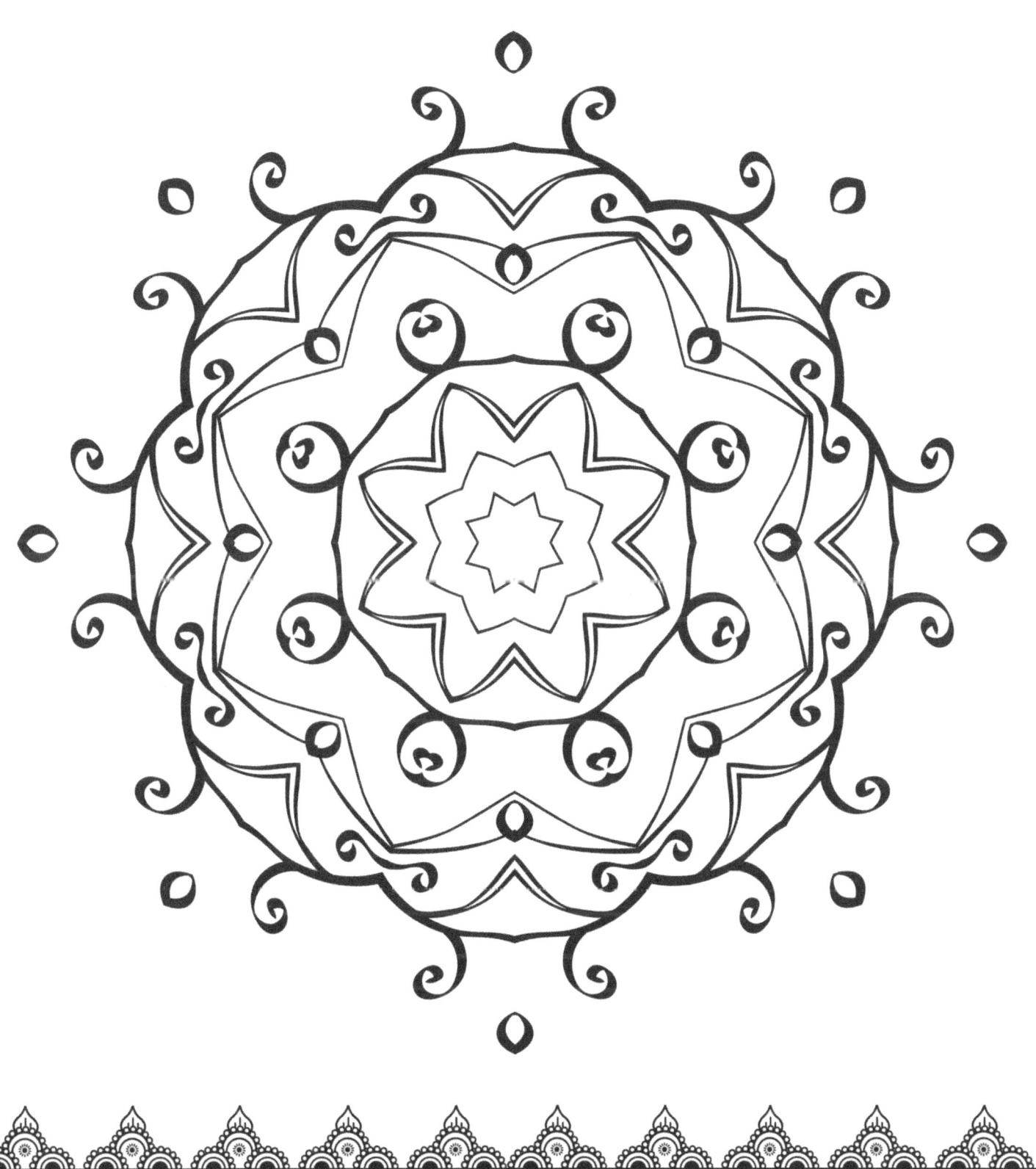

Circular symmetric mandala

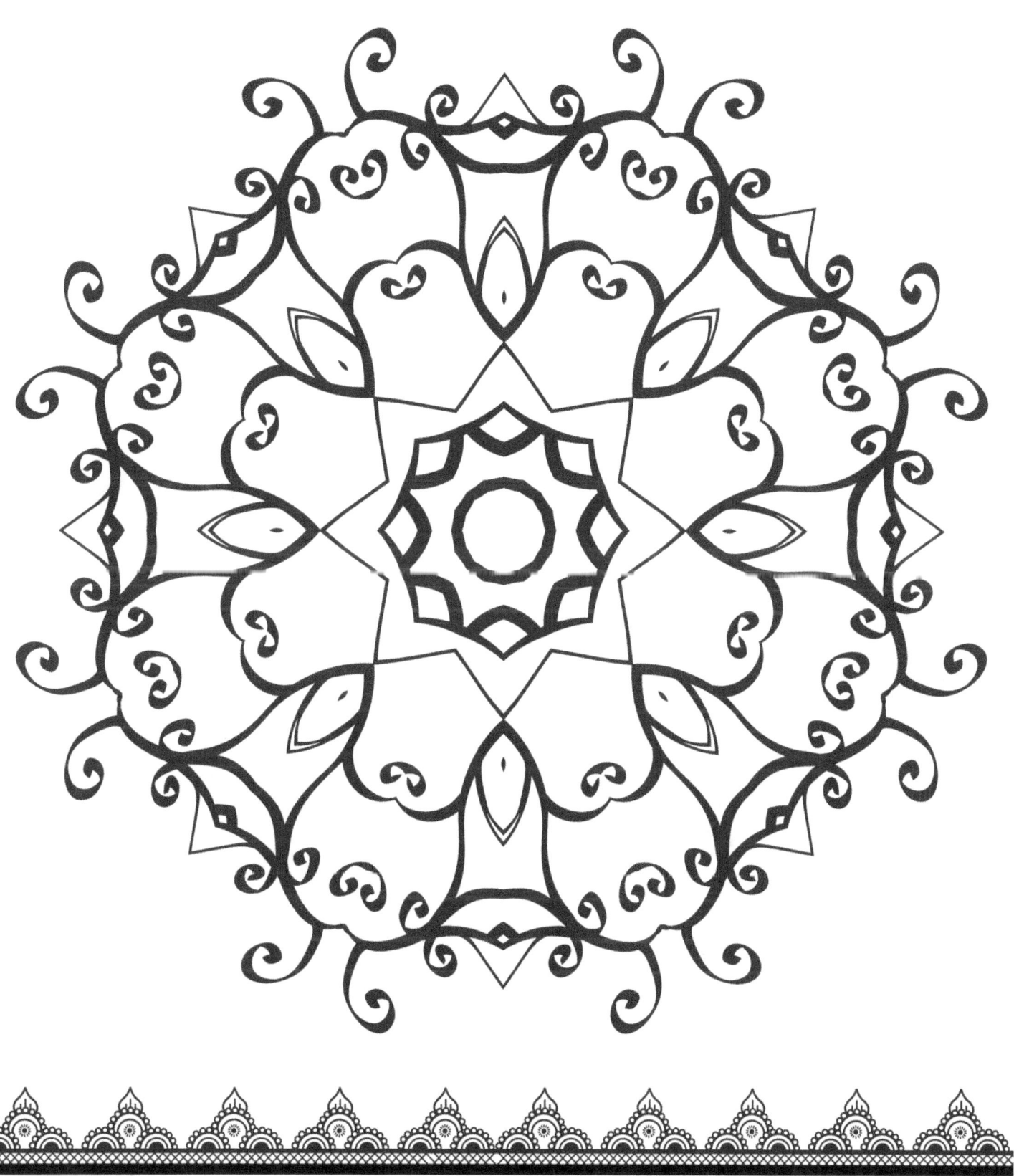

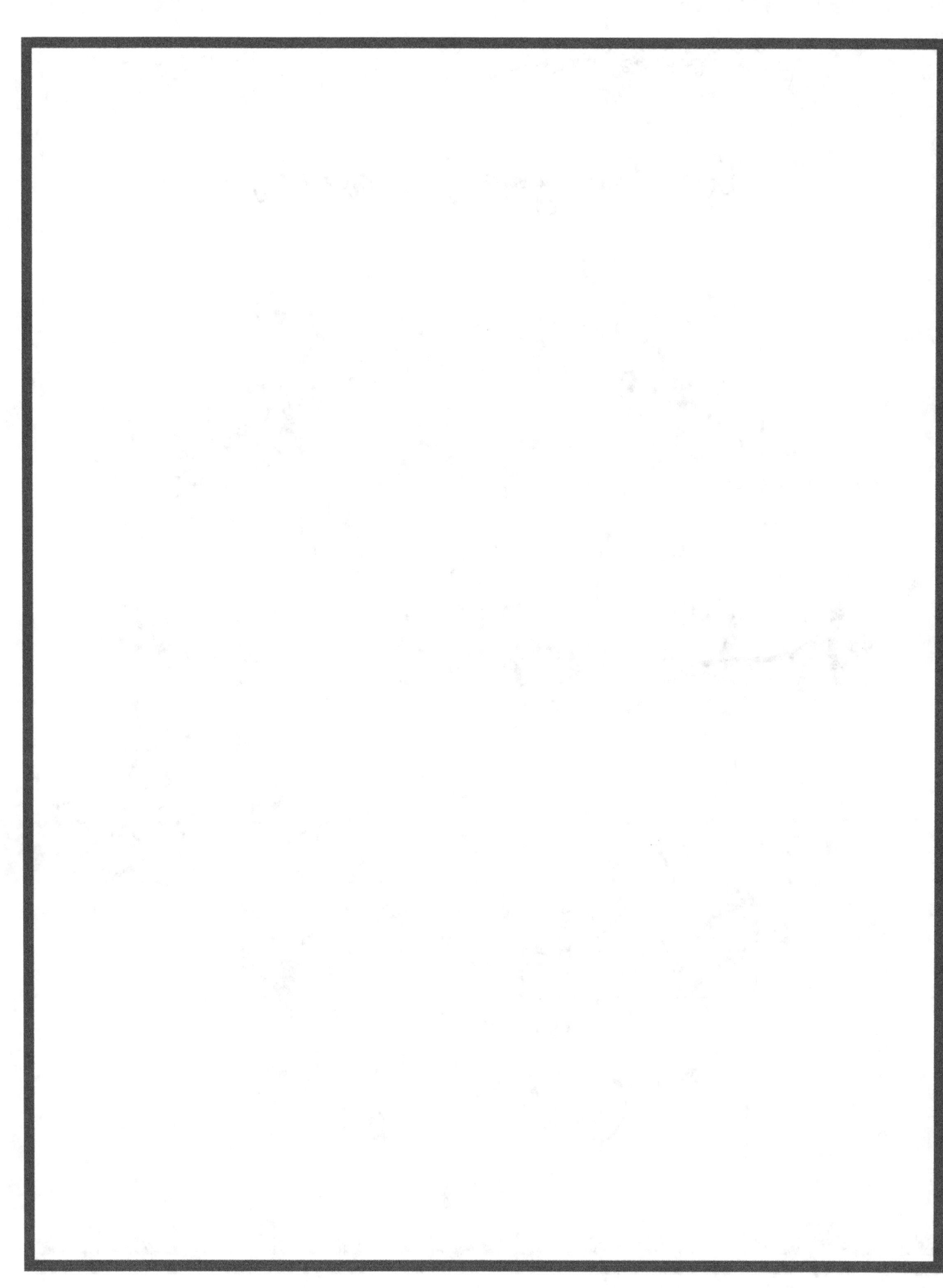

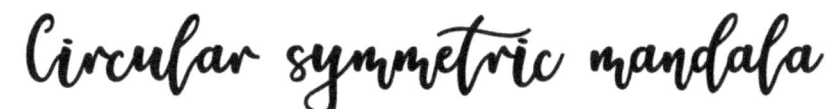

Circular symmetric mandala

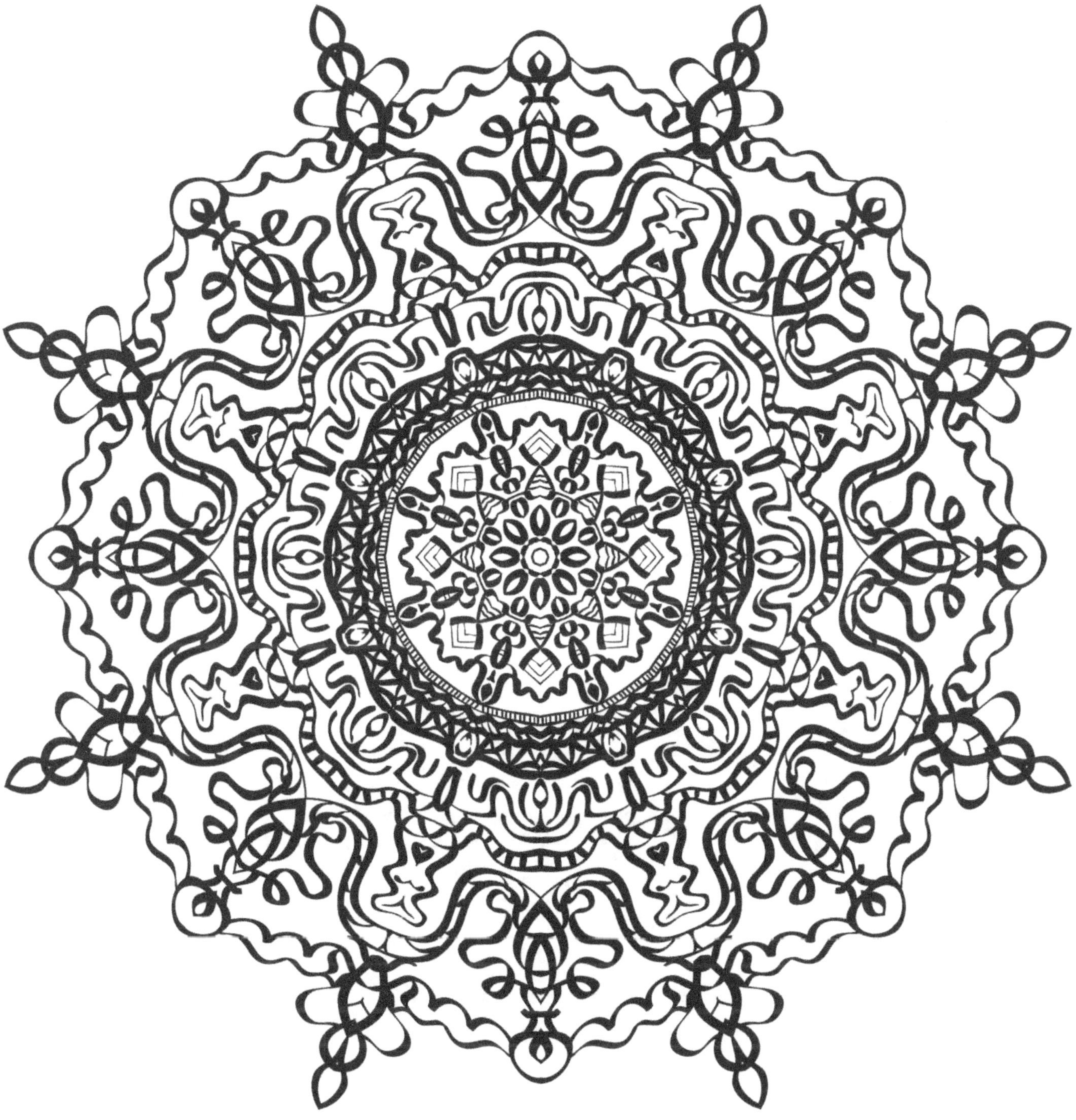

Circular symmetric mandala

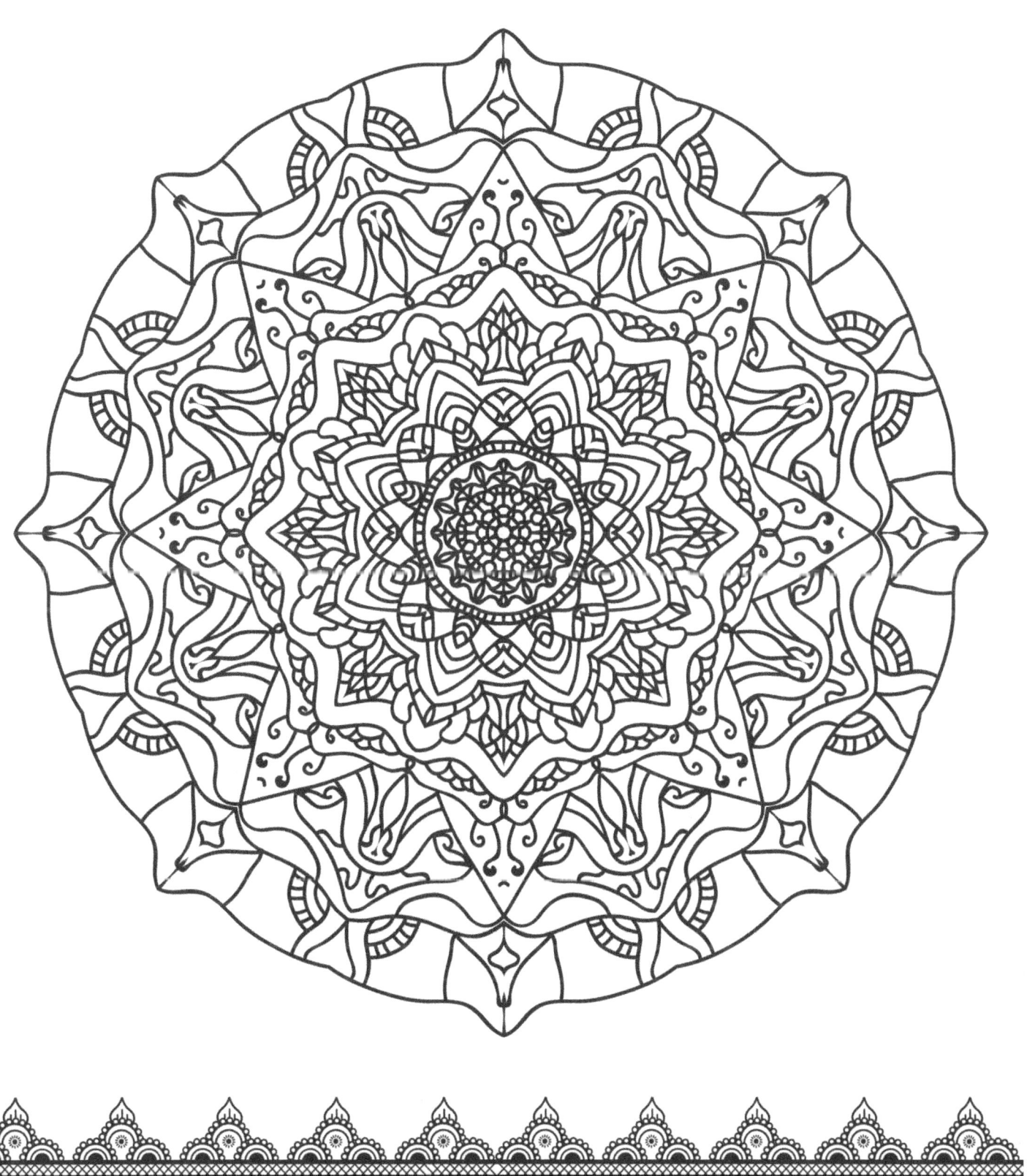

Circular symmetric mandala

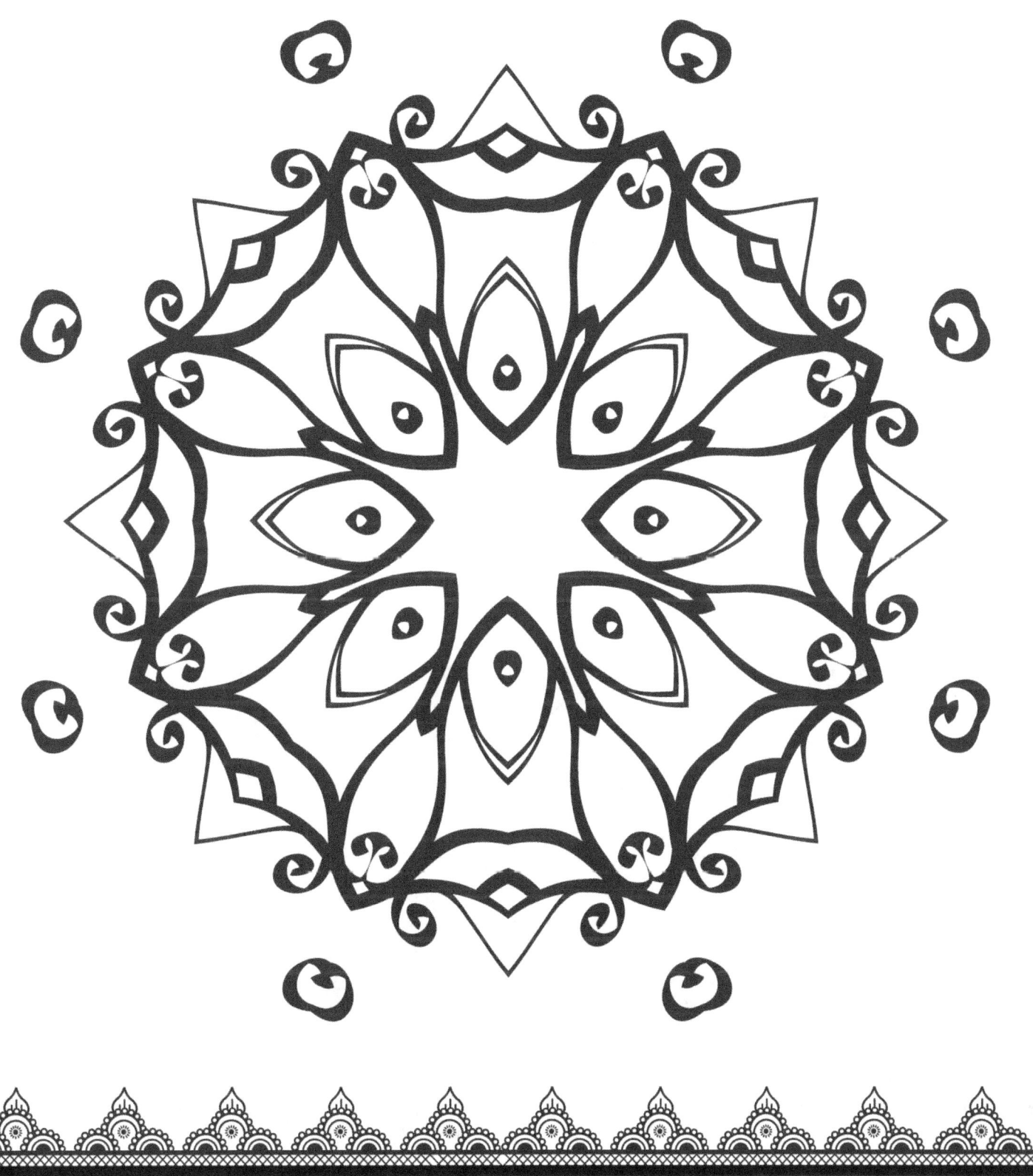

Circular symmetric mandala

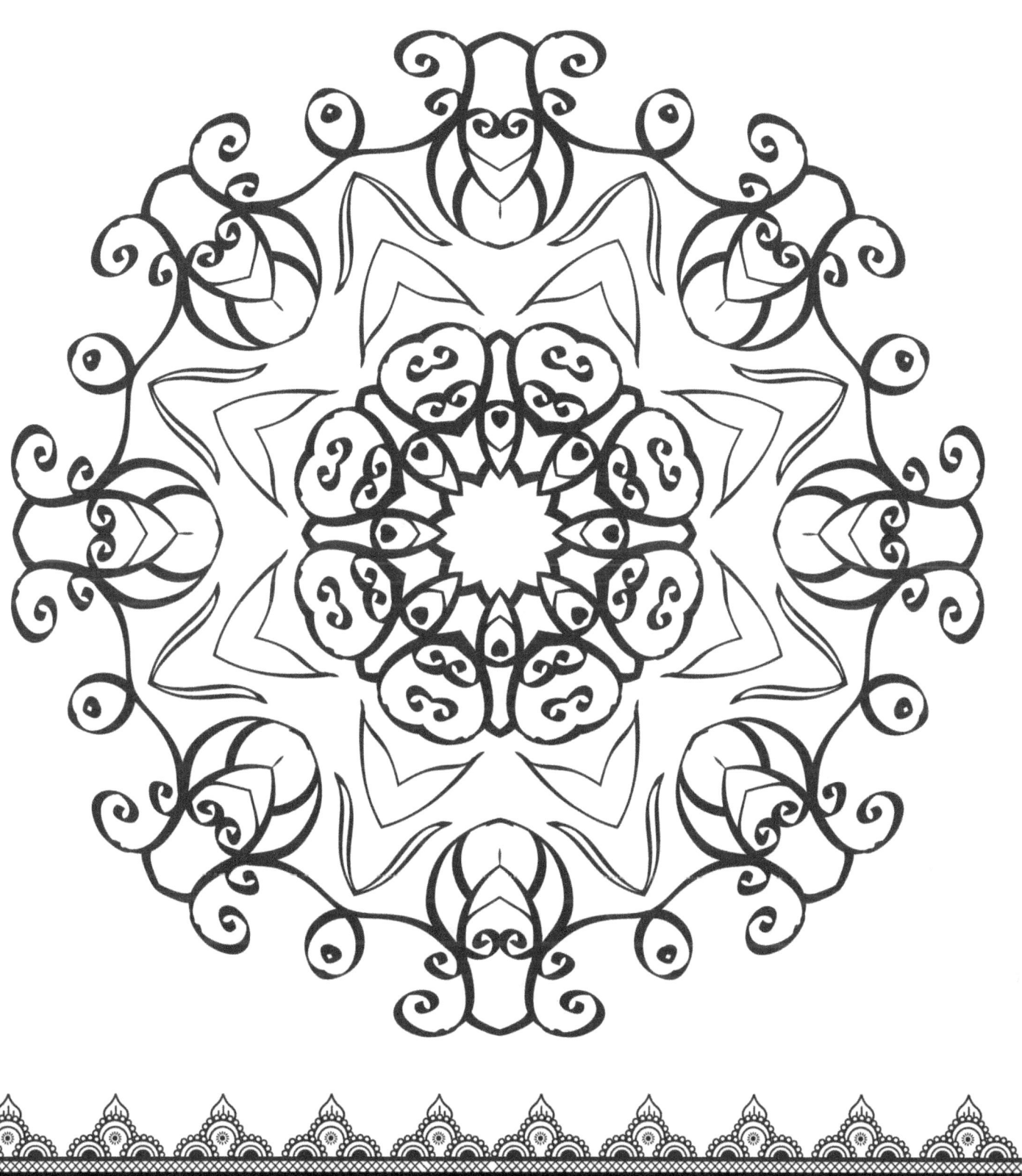

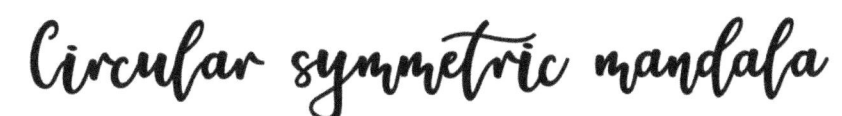

Circular symmetric mandala

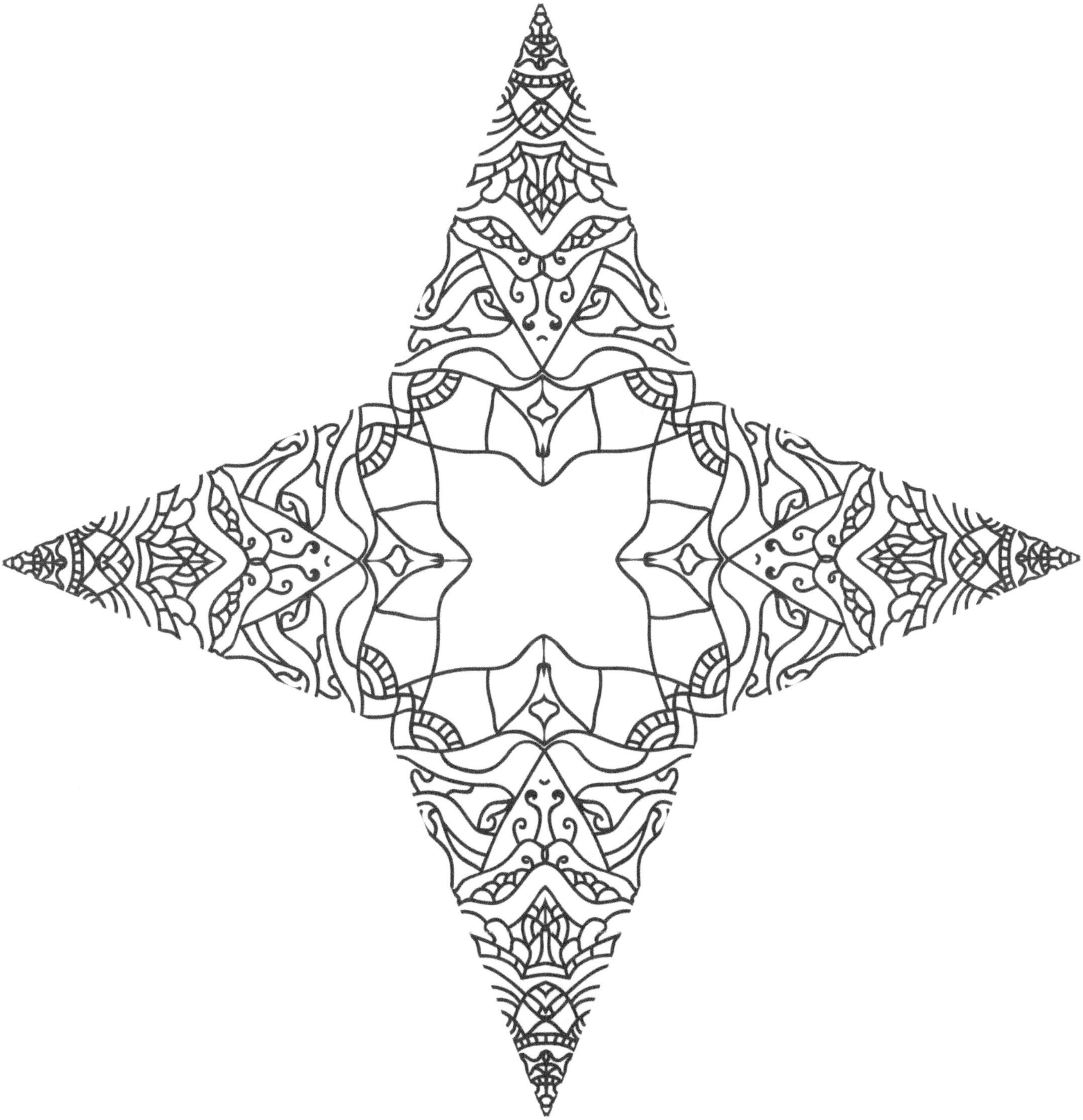

Circular symmetric mandala

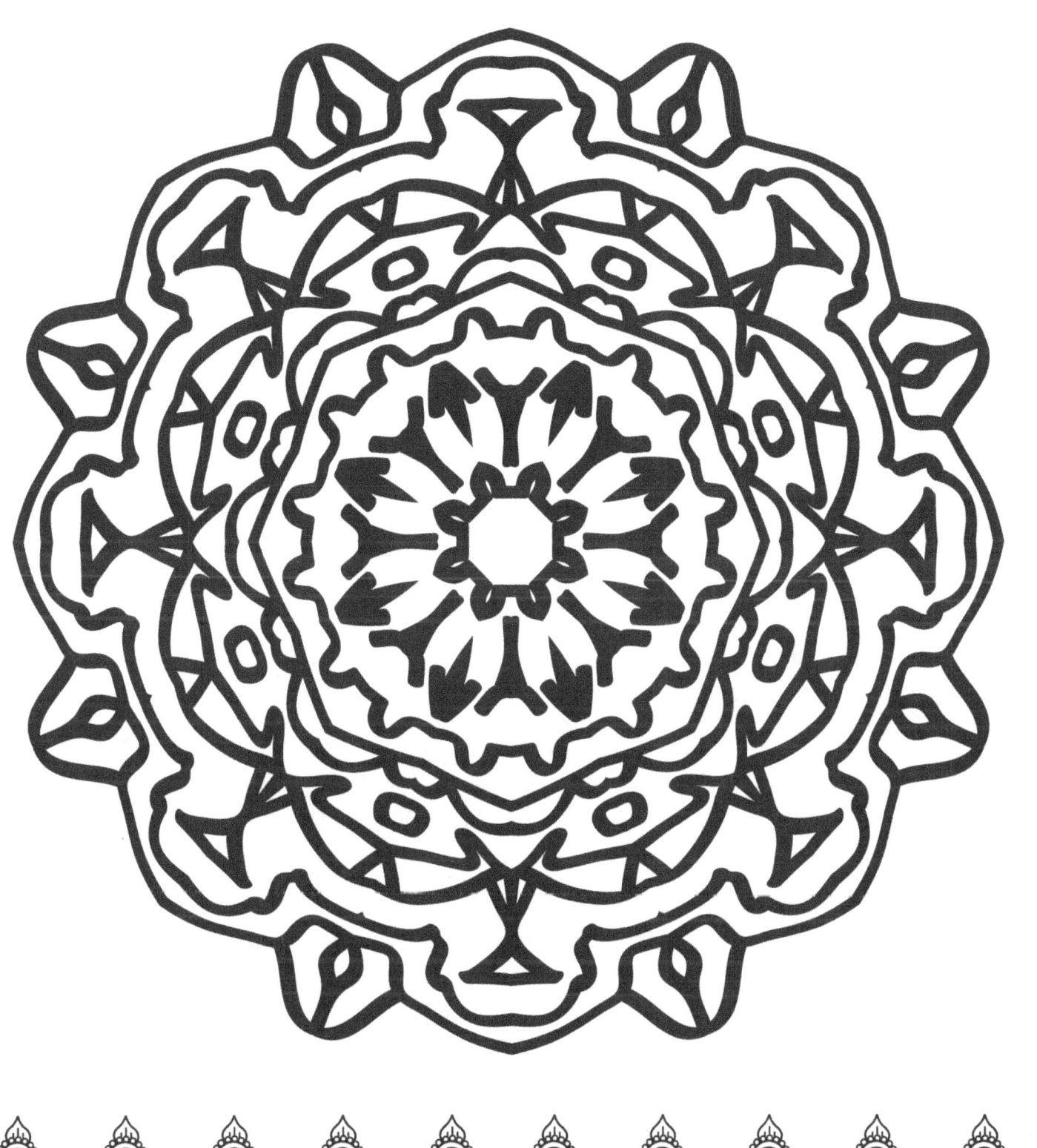

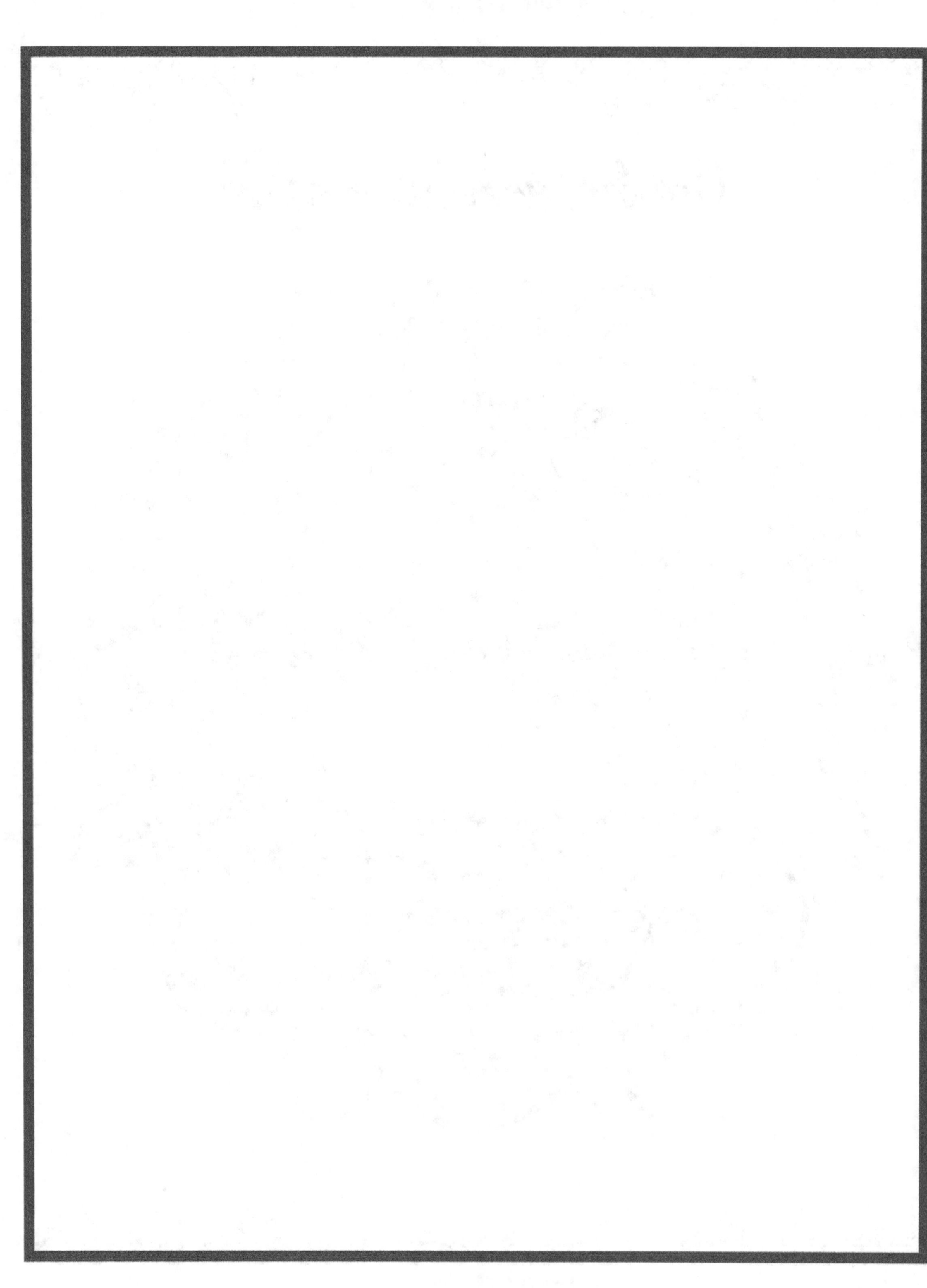

Macaw mandala zentangle and tshirt

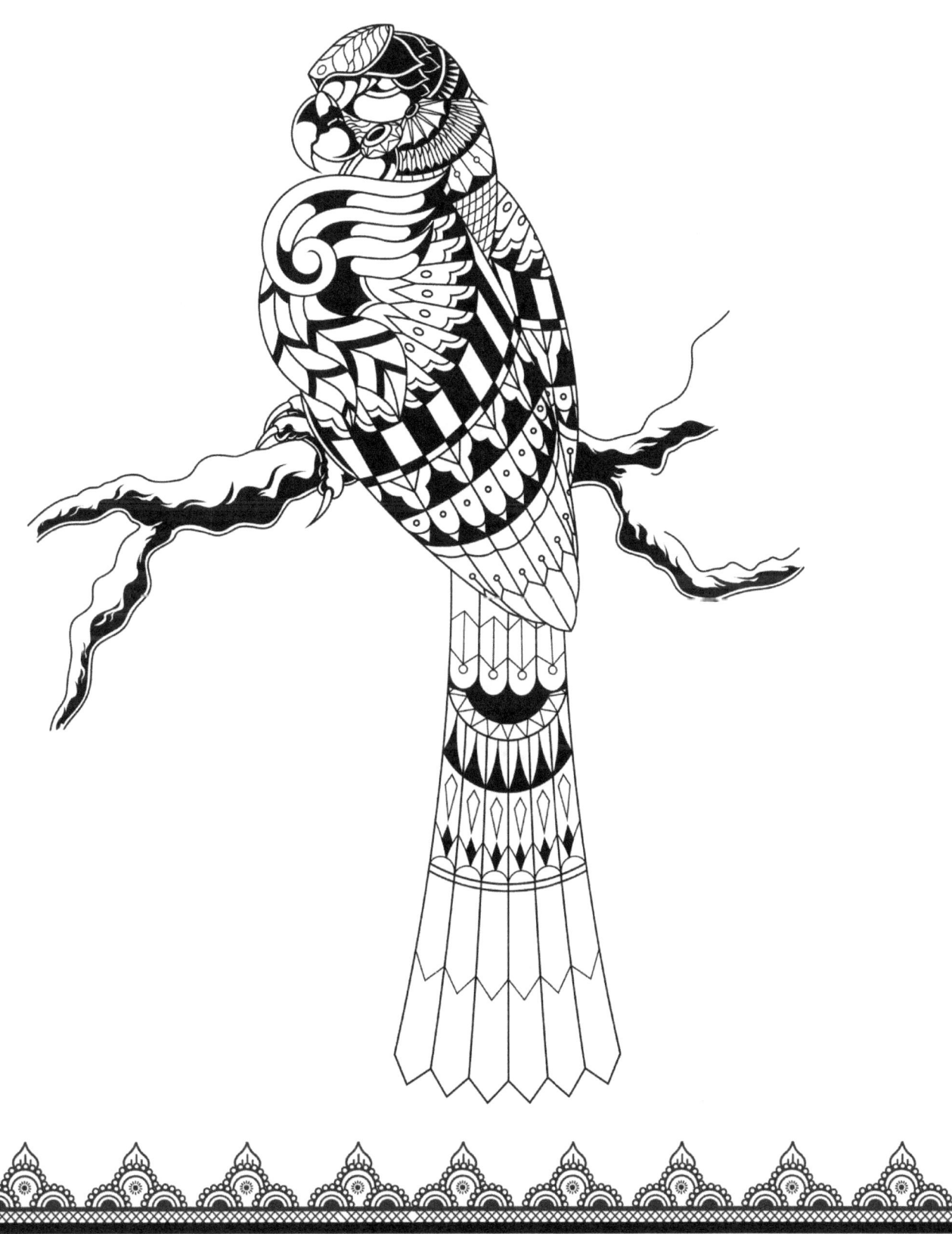

Butterfly mandala

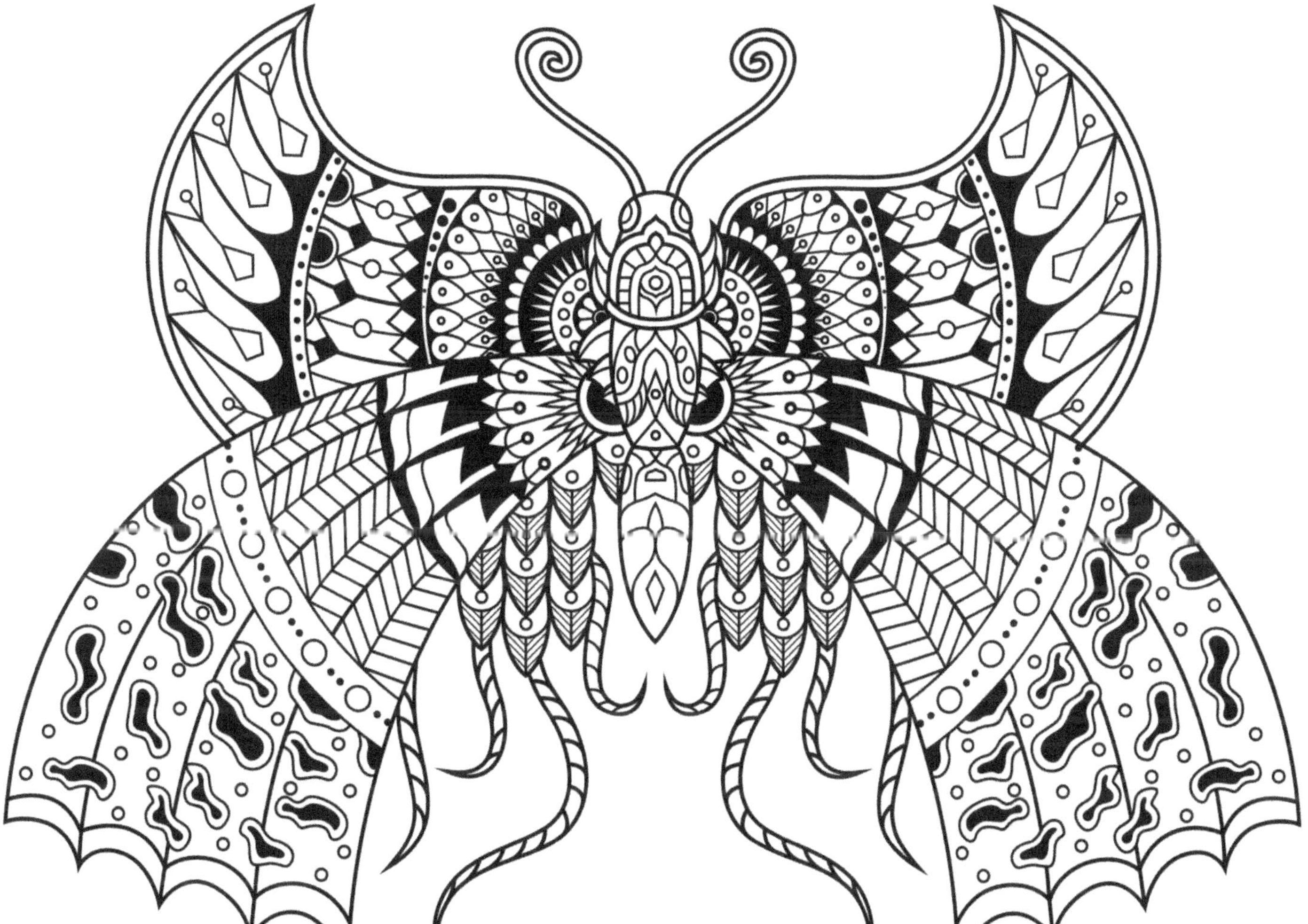

Butterfly mandala

www.ingramcontent.com/pod-product-compliance
Lightning Source LLC
Chambersburg PA
CBHW080624220526
45467CB00011B/3352